Quiet Time for the Bride-to-be

Refresh your soul as you plan your wedding

Published in the USA.
First Edition March 1, 2018.

Scripture verses are paraphrased from the King James version of the Holy Bible -Public Domain.
Cover and interior design, salutation, coloring pages, scripture selection and arrangement by Cathy Idowu

ISBN 978-0- 9801484-2- 8 Paperback.

For contact and permissions: journalsbycatherine@gmail.com
Ritequest Publishing
Florida, USA

Dear *Bride-to-be*, congratulations on your big news and blessings to you and your groom! This prayer journal has been designed to help you come confidently before God in prayer as you plan your wedding. The first recorded miracle that Jesus did was at a wedding in Cana. The wine had run out during the reception, and Jesus' mother, Mary, came boldly before her son to share the situation with Him. Jesus honored her boldness and turned water into wine. The master of ceremony testified that this wine was better tasting than the previous wine served! As you bring all your wedding plans and situations before the Lord Jesus in prayer, have an expectation that the outcomes will be far better and sweeter than if you had done it alone in your own strength. Furthermore, prayerful planning provides an opportunity to see tangible expressions of God's love for you as He answers specific prayers. This serves to increase your faith in Him.

This prayer journal has been designed to help you with your prayer and devotional life, as you plan. Hopefully, it will end up as a keepsake full of treasured memories. God always wants us to keep a record of His faithfulness to us and this journal provides you with an opportunity to do just that.

Contents and use of this journal

- A love story page.

- A page to journal the proposal.

- A wedding checklist surrounded with faith-building scriptures that will help launch you into prayer during your planning. This list is not exhaustive - extra spaces are included for you to write in your more specific plans.

- Scripture-themed prayer points for you and your groom. Of course, you'll probably have unique ones, including God's promises that are special to both of you. The idea is to pray the scriptures.

- The main journal section is divided into 6 days. Each day includes a "Word for my soul" section —use any devotional, message, or Bible-in-a-year reading, and journal what you sense God is saying to you; An "I'm thankful for" section —include points of gratitude and answered prayer here; A "Prayer focus/ request" section — include prayer points from the checklist provided, and other situations unique to you and your groom; A "Letting go of this anxious thought" section— Here's your opportunity to exercise your faith by letting go of anxieties over preparation, and letting God handle it. At the end of your six days, you have two pages for your seventh day, giving you plenty of space for weekly reflections, ideas, thoughts, etc. In total, you have six months or 26 weeks worth of journaling pages.

- Finally, there's a little bit of fun in the last one dozen pages of this journal: Adult coloring for some stress relief! The quick and simple designs have your busy schedule in mind, while at the same time providing an opportunity to help you meditate on faith-building truths. The back of each of these pages is blank, in case you decide to cut out your colored pieces to frame. They're conveniently sized to fit into a 5 x7 picture frame. Blank note cards are included on the last pages for your personalized quotes and scriptures.

Once again, congratulations!

This journal belongs to:

_ _

Date I said "Yes." _ _ _ _ _ _ _ _ _ _

Date I'll say "I do." _ _ _ _ _ _ _ _ _

To be married:

"Commit your way to the Lord; Trust also in Him, and He shall bring it to pass."

Psalm 37:5

I have found
the one whom
my soul loves
Song of Solomon 3:4

The Proposal

Praying thru' my wedding checklist...

Commit your way to the Lord; Trust also in Him; and He shall bring it to pass.

Psalm 37:5

I will instruct you and teach you, showing you the best path to take.

Psalm 32:8

Teach us to number our days that we may apply our hearts unto wisdom.

Psalm 90:12

Budget, Family, Volunteers

Venues & Dates Reserved

Planner, Vendors - Online/Local

Officiant/Ministers/Counselor

Dress - Bride, Groom, & Party

Theme, Invitation, Website

Guests, Hotels/ Travel, RSVPs

Other________________________

Ask, and it shall be given to you; seek, and you will find; knock, and the door will be opened for you.

Matthew 7:7

Be anxious for nothing, but by prayer and supplication, with thanksgiving, make all your requests known to God; and the peace of God which surpasses all understanding, will guard your hearts and minds,s, through Christ Jesus.

Philippians 4:6-7

Dear Father,
I pray for us
That...

We might live in the way You *require* of us: Doing *justice*, loving *kindness*, and walking *humbly* with You.

Micah 6:8

You will *satisfy* us early with *Your love*, that we may *rejoice* and be *glad* all our days.

Psalm 90:14

We will have a *deep love* for *each other*

1 Peter 4:8,

We will speak the *truth* to each other, *in love*.

Ephesians 4:15

Your *favor* will rest *upon us* and You will *establish* the work of *our hands* for us.

Psalm 90:17

We will understand Your *plans* for us: *to prosper* us, and *not to harm* us; to give us a *future* and *a hope*.

Jeremiah 29:11

Love is patient,
love is kind. Love
does not envy, nor is it
proud or rude.
It does not insist on
its own way, nor
does it get easily
offended. It does not
harbor malice.
It does not rejoice in
wrong-doing, but
rejoices in truth.
It bears all things,
believes all things,
hopes all things, and
endures all things.

LOVE NEVER FAILS.

1 Corinthians 13:4-8

Today's word for my soul

Date:

I'm thankful for...

Letting go of this anxious thought

Prayer focus & requests

Today's word for my soul

Date:

I'm thankful for...

Letting go of this anxious thought

Prayer focus & requests

Today's word for my soul

Date:

I'm thankful for...

Letting go of this anxious thought

Prayer focus & requests

Today's word for my soul

Date:

I'm thankful for...

Letting go of this anxious thought

Prayer focus & requests

Today's word for my soul

Date:

I'm thankful for...

Letting go of this anxious thought

Prayer focus & requests

Today's word for my soul

Date:

I'm thankful for...

Letting go of this anxious thought

Prayer focus & requests

Gratitude
Hopes
Dreams
Quotes
Verses
Poems
Lyrics
Thoughts
Messages

ReflectionS

Week#_______

Today's word for my soul

Date:

I'm thankful for...

Letting go of this anxious thought

Prayer focus & requests

Today's word for my soul

Date:

I'm thankful for...

Letting go of this anxious thought

Prayer focus & requests

Today's word for my soul

Date:

I'm thankful for...

Letting go of this anxious thought

Prayer focus & requests

Today's word for my soul

Date:

I'm thankful for...

Letting go of this anxious thought

Prayer focus & requests

Today's word for my soul

Date:

I'm thankful for...

Letting go of this anxious thought

Prayer focus & requests

Today's word for my soul

Date:

I'm thankful for...

Letting go of this anxious thought

Prayer focus & requests

Gratitude
Hopes
Dreams
Quotes
Verses
Poems
Lyrics
Thoughts
Messages

Reflections

Week#______

Today's word for my soul

Date:

I'm thankful for...

Letting go of this anxious thought

Prayer focus & requests

Today's word for my soul

Date:

I'm thankful for...

Letting go of this anxious thought

Prayer focus & requests

Today's word for my soul

Date:

I'm thankful for...

Letting go of this anxious thought

Prayer focus & requests

Today's word for my soul

Date:

I'm thankful for...

Letting go of this anxious thought

Prayer focus & requests

Today's word for my soul

Date:

I'm thankful for...

Letting go of this anxious thought

Prayer focus & requests

Today's word for my soul

Date:

I'm thankful for...

Letting go of this anxious thought

Prayer focus & requests

Gratitude
Hopes
Dreams
Quotes
Verses
Poems
Lyrics
Thoughts
Messages

ReflectionS

Week#_______

Today's word for my soul

Date:

I'm thankful for...

Letting go of this anxious thought

Prayer focus & requests

Today's word for my soul

Date:

I'm thankful for...

Letting go of this anxious thought

Prayer focus & requests

Today's word for my soul

Date:

I'm thankful for...

Letting go of this anxious thought

Prayer focus & requests

Today's word for my soul

Date:

I'm thankful for...

Letting go of this anxious thought

Prayer focus & requests

Today's word for my soul

Date:

I'm thankful for...

Letting go of this anxious thought

Prayer focus & requests

Today's word for my soul

Date:

I'm thankful for...

Letting go of this anxious thought

Prayer focus & requests

Gratitude
Hopes
Dreams
Quotes
Verses
Poems
Lyrics
Thoughts
Messages

ReflectionS

Week#________

Today's word for my soul

Date:

I'm thankful for...

Letting go of this anxious thought

Prayer focus & requests

Today's word for my soul

Date:

I'm thankful for...

Letting go of this anxious thought

Prayer focus & requests

Today's word for my soul

Date:

I'm thankful for...

Letting go of this anxious thought

Prayer focus & requests

Today's word for my soul

Date:

I'm thankful for...

Letting go of this anxious thought

Prayer focus & requests

Today's word for my soul

Date:

I'm thankful for...

Letting go of this anxious thought

Prayer focus & requests

Today's word for my soul

Date:

I'm thankful for...

Letting go of this anxious thought

Prayer focus & requests

Gratitude
Hopes
Dreams
Quotes
Verses
Poems
Lyrics
Thoughts
Messages

ReflectionS

Week#________

Today's word for my soul

Date:

I'm thankful for...

Letting go of this anxious thought

Prayer focus & requests

Today's word for my soul

Date:

I'm thankful for...

Letting go of this anxious thought

Prayer focus & requests

Today's word for my soul

Date:

I'm thankful for...

Letting go of this anxious thought

Prayer focus & requests

Today's word for my soul

Date:

I'm thankful for...

Letting go of this anxious thought

Prayer focus & requests

Today's word for my soul

Date:

I'm thankful for...

Letting go of this anxious thought

Prayer focus & requests

Today's word for my soul

Date:

I'm thankful for...

Letting go of this anxious thought

Prayer focus & requests

Gratitude
Hopes
Dreams
Quotes
Verses
Poems
Lyrics
Thoughts
Messages

ReflectionS

Week#_______

Today's word for my soul

Date:

I'm thankful for...

Letting go of this anxious thought

Prayer focus & requests

Today's word for my soul

Date:

I'm thankful for...

Letting go of this anxious thought

Prayer focus & requests

Today's word for my soul

Date:

I'm thankful for...

Letting go of this anxious thought

Prayer focus & requests

Today's word for my soul

Date:

I'm thankful for...

Letting go of this anxious thought

Prayer focus & requests

Today's word for my soul

Date:

I'm thankful for...

Letting go of this anxious thought

Prayer focus & requests

Today's word for my soul

Date:

I'm thankful for...

Letting go of this anxious thought

Prayer focus & requests

Gratitude
Hopes
Dreams
Quotes
Verses
Poems
Lyrics
Thoughts
Messages

ReflectionS

Week#______

Today's word for my soul

Date:

I'm thankful for...

Letting go of this anxious thought

Prayer focus & requests

Today's word for my soul

Date:

I'm thankful for...

Letting go of this anxious thought

Prayer focus & requests

Today's word for my soul

Date:

I'm thankful for...

Letting go of this anxious thought

Prayer focus & requests

Today's word for my soul

Date:

I'm thankful for...

Letting go of this anxious thought

Prayer focus & requests

Today's word for my soul

Date:

I'm thankful for...

Letting go of this anxious thought

Prayer focus & requests

Today's word for my soul

Date:

I'm thankful for...

Letting go of this anxious thought

Prayer focus & requests

Gratitude
Hopes
Dreams
Quotes
Verses
Poems
Lyrics
Thoughts
Messages

ReflectionS

Week#_______

Today's word for my soul

Date:

I'm thankful for...

Letting go of this anxious thought

Prayer focus & requests

Today's word for my soul

Date:

I'm thankful for...

Letting go of this anxious thought

Prayer focus & requests

Today's word for my soul

Date:

I'm thankful for...

Letting go of this anxious thought

Prayer focus & requests

Today's word for my soul

Date:

I'm thankful for...

Letting go of this anxious thought

Prayer focus & requests

Today's word for my soul

Date:

I'm thankful for...

Letting go of this anxious thought

Prayer focus & requests

Today's word for my soul

Date:

I'm thankful for...

Letting go of this anxious thought

Prayer focus & requests

Gratitude
Hopes
Dreams
Quotes
Verses
Poems
Lyrics
Thoughts
Messages

ReflectionS

Week#________

Today's word for my soul

Date:

I'm thankful for...

Letting go of this anxious thought

Prayer focus & requests

Today's word for my soul

Date:

I'm thankful for...

Letting go of this anxious thought

Prayer focus & requests

Today's word for my soul

Date:

I'm thankful for...

Letting go of this anxious thought

Prayer focus & requests

Today's word for my soul

Date:

I'm thankful for...

Letting go of this anxious thought

Prayer focus & requests

Today's word for my soul

Date:

I'm thankful for...

Letting go of this anxious thought

Prayer focus & requests

Today's word for my soul

Date:

I'm thankful for...

Letting go of this anxious thought

Prayer focus & requests

Gratitude
Hopes
Dreams
Quotes
Verses
Poems
Lyrics
Thoughts
Messages

ReflectionS

Week#________

Today's word for my soul

Date:

I'm thankful for...

Letting go of this anxious thought

Prayer focus & requests

Today's word for my soul

Date:

I'm thankful for...

Letting go of this anxious thought

Prayer focus & requests

Today's word for my soul

Date:

I'm thankful for...

Letting go of this anxious thought

Prayer focus & requests

Today's word for my soul

Date:

I'm thankful for...

Letting go of this anxious thought

Prayer focus & requests

Today's word for my soul

Date:

I'm thankful for...

Letting go of this anxious thought

Prayer focus & requests

Today's word for my soul

Date:

I'm thankful for...

Letting go of this anxious thought

Prayer focus & requests

Gratitude
Hopes
Dreams
Quotes
Verses
Poems
Lyrics
Thoughts
Messages

ReflectionS

Week#________

Today's word for my soul

Date:

I'm thankful for...

Letting go of this anxious thought

Prayer focus & requests

Today's word for my soul

Date:

I'm thankful for...

Letting go of this anxious thought

Prayer focus & requests

Today's word for my soul

Date:

I'm thankful for...

Letting go of this anxious thought

Prayer focus & requests

Today's word for my soul

Date:

I'm thankful for...

Letting go of this anxious thought

Prayer focus & requests

Today's word for my soul

Date:

I'm thankful for...

Letting go of this anxious thought

Prayer focus & requests

Today's word for my soul

Date:

I'm thankful for...

Letting go of this anxious thought

Prayer focus & requests

Gratitude
Hopes
Dreams
Quotes
Verses
Poems
Lyrics
Thoughts
Messages

ReflectionS

Week#________

Today's word for my soul

Date:

I'm thankful for...

Letting go of this anxious thought

Prayer focus & requests

Today's word for my soul

Date:

I'm thankful for...

Letting go of this anxious thought

Prayer focus & requests

Today's word for my soul

Date:

I'm thankful for...

Letting go of this anxious thought

Prayer focus & requests

Today's word for my soul

Date:

I'm thankful for...

Letting go of this anxious thought

Prayer focus & requests

Today's word for my soul

Date:

I'm thankful for...

Letting go of this anxious thought

Prayer focus & requests

Today's word for my soul

Date:

I'm thankful for...

Letting go of this anxious thought

Prayer focus & requests

Gratitude
Hopes
Dreams
Quotes
Verses
Poems
Lyrics
Thoughts
Messages

ReflectionS

Week#_______

Today's word for my soul

Date:

I'm thankful for...

Letting go of this anxious thought

Prayer focus & requests

Today's word for my soul

Date:

I'm thankful for...

Letting go of this anxious thought

Prayer focus & requests

Today's word for my soul

Date:

I'm thankful for...

Letting go of this anxious thought

Prayer focus & requests

Today's word for my soul

Date:

I'm thankful for...

Letting go of this anxious thought

Prayer focus & requests

Today's word for my soul

Date:

I'm thankful for...

Letting go of this anxious thought

Prayer focus & requests

Today's word for my soul

Date:

I'm thankful for...

Letting go of this anxious thought

Prayer focus & requests

Gratitude
Hopes
Dreams
Quotes
Verses
Poems
Lyrics
Thoughts
Messages

ReflectionS

Week#_______

Today's word for my soul

Date:

I'm thankful for...

Letting go of this anxious thought

Prayer focus & requests

Today's word for my soul

Date:

I'm thankful for...

Letting go of this anxious thought

Prayer focus & requests

Today's word for my soul

Date:

I'm thankful for...

Letting go of this anxious thought

Prayer focus & requests

Today's word for my soul

Date:

I'm thankful for...

Letting go of this anxious thought

Prayer focus & requests

Today's word for my soul

Date:

I'm thankful for...

Letting go of this anxious thought

Prayer focus & requests

Today's word for my soul

Date:

I'm thankful for...

Letting go of this anxious thought

Prayer focus & requests

Gratitude
Hopes
Dreams
Quotes
Verses
Poems
Lyrics
Thoughts
Messages

ReflectionS

Week#________

Today's word for my soul

Date:

I'm thankful for...

Letting go of this anxious thought

Prayer focus & requests

Today's word for my soul

Date:

I'm thankful for...

Letting go of this anxious thought

Prayer focus & requests

Today's word for my soul

Date:

I'm thankful for...

Letting go of this anxious thought

Prayer focus & requests

Today's word for my soul

Date:

I'm thankful for...

Letting go of this anxious thought

Prayer focus & requests

Today's word for my soul

Date:

I'm thankful for...

Letting go of this anxious thought

Prayer focus & requests

Today's word for my soul

Date:

I'm thankful for...

Letting go of this anxious thought

Prayer focus & requests

Gratitude
Hopes
Dreams
Quotes
Verses
Poems
Lyrics
Thoughts
Messages

ReflectionS

Week#________

Today's word for my soul

Date:

I'm thankful for...

Letting go of this anxious thought

Prayer focus & requests

Today's word for my soul

Date:

I'm thankful for...

Letting go of this anxious thought

Prayer focus & requests

Today's word for my soul

Date:

I'm thankful for...

Letting go of this anxious thought

Prayer focus & requests

Today's word for my soul

Date:

I'm thankful for...

Letting go of this anxious thought

Prayer focus & requests

Today's word for my soul

Date:

I'm thankful for...

Letting go of this anxious thought

Prayer focus & requests

Today's word for my soul

Date:

I'm thankful for...

Letting go of this anxious thought

Prayer focus & requests

Gratitude
Hopes
Dreams
Quotes
Verses
Poems
Lyrics
Thoughts
Messages

ReflectionS

Week#________

Today's word for my soul

Date:

I'm thankful for...

Letting go of this anxious thought

Prayer focus & requests

Today's word for my soul

Date:

I'm thankful for...

Letting go of this anxious thought

Prayer focus & requests

Today's word for my soul

Date:

I'm thankful for...

Letting go of this anxious thought

Prayer focus & requests

Today's word for my soul

Date:

I'm thankful for...

Letting go of this anxious thought

Prayer focus & requests

Today's word for my soul

Date:

I'm thankful for...

Letting go of this anxious thought

Prayer focus & requests

Today's word for my soul

Date:

I'm thankful for...

Letting go of this anxious thought

Prayer focus & requests

Gratitude
Hopes
Dreams
Quotes
Verses
Poems
Lyrics
Thoughts
Messages

ReflectionS

Week#_______

Today's word for my soul

Date:

I'm thankful for...

Letting go of this anxious thought

Prayer focus & requests

Today's word for my soul

Date:

I'm thankful for...

Letting go of this anxious thought

Prayer focus & requests

Today's word for my soul

Date:

I'm thankful for...

Letting go of this anxious thought

Prayer focus & requests

Today's word for my soul

Date:

I'm thankful for...

Letting go of this anxious thought

Prayer focus & requests

Today's word for my soul

Date:

I'm thankful for...

Letting go of this anxious thought

Prayer focus & requests

Today's word for my soul

Date:

I'm thankful for...

Letting go of this anxious thought

Prayer focus & requests

Gratitude
Hopes
Dreams
Quotes
Verses
Poems
Lyrics
Thoughts
Messages

ReflectionS

Week#________

Today's word for my soul

Date:

I'm thankful for...

Letting go of this anxious thought

Prayer focus & requests

Today's word for my soul

Date:

I'm thankful for...

Letting go of this anxious thought

Prayer focus & requests

Today's word for my soul

Date:

I'm thankful for...

Letting go of this anxious thought

Prayer focus & requests

Today's word for my soul

Date:

I'm thankful for...

Letting go of this anxious thought

Prayer focus & requests

Today's word for my soul

Date:

I'm thankful for...

Letting go of this anxious thought

Prayer focus & requests

Today's word for my soul

Date:

I'm thankful for...

Letting go of this anxious thought

Prayer focus & requests

Gratitude
Hopes
Dreams
Quotes
Verses
Poems
Lyrics
Thoughts
Messages

ReflectionS

Week#________

Today's word for my soul

Date:

I'm thankful for...

Letting go of this anxious thought

Prayer focus & requests

Today's word for my soul

Date:

I'm thankful for...

Letting go of this anxious thought

Prayer focus & requests

Today's word for my soul

Date:

I'm thankful for...

Letting go of this anxious thought

Prayer focus & requests

Today's word for my soul

Date:

I'm thankful for...

Letting go of this anxious thought

Prayer focus & requests

Today's word for my soul

Date:

I'm thankful for...

Letting go of this anxious thought

Prayer focus & requests

Today's word for my soul

Date:

I'm thankful for...

Letting go of this anxious thought

Prayer focus & requests

Gratitude
Hopes
Dreams
Quotes
Verses
Poems
Lyrics
Thoughts
Messages

ReflectionS

Week#_______

Today's word for my soul

Date:

I'm thankful for...

Letting go of this anxious thought

Prayer focus & requests

Today's word for my soul

Date:

I'm thankful for...

Letting go of this anxious thought

Prayer focus & requests

Today's word for my soul

Date:

I'm thankful for...

Letting go of this anxious thought

Prayer focus & requests

Today's word for my soul

Date:

I'm thankful for...

Letting go of this anxious thought

Prayer focus & requests

Today's word for my soul

Date:

I'm thankful for...

Letting go of this anxious thought

Prayer focus & requests

Today's word for my soul

Date:

I'm thankful for...

Letting go of this anxious thought

Prayer focus & requests

Gratitude
Hopes
Dreams
Quotes
Verses
Poems
Lyrics
Thoughts
Messages

ReflectionS

Week#________

Today's word for my soul

Date:

I'm thankful for...

Letting go of this anxious thought

Prayer focus & requests

Today's word for my soul

Date:

I'm thankful for...

Letting go of this anxious thought

Prayer focus & requests

Today's word for my soul

Date:

I'm thankful for...

Letting go of this anxious thought

Prayer focus & requests

Today's word for my soul

Date:

I'm thankful for...

Letting go of this anxious thought

Prayer focus & requests

Today's word for my soul

Date:

I'm thankful for...

Letting go of this anxious thought

Prayer focus & requests

Today's word for my soul

Date:

I'm thankful for...

Letting go of this anxious thought

Prayer focus & requests

Gratitude
Hopes
Dreams
Quotes
Verses
Poems
Lyrics
Thoughts
Messages

ReflectionS

Week#________

Today's word for my soul

Date:

I'm thankful for...

Letting go of this anxious thought

Prayer focus & requests

Today's word for my soul

Date:

I'm thankful for...

Letting go of this anxious thought

Prayer focus & requests

Today's word for my soul

Date:

I'm thankful for...

Letting go of this anxious thought

Prayer focus & requests

Today's word for my soul

Date:

I'm thankful for...

Letting go of this anxious thought

Prayer focus & requests

Today's word for my soul

Date:

I'm thankful for...

Letting go of this anxious thought

Prayer focus & requests

Today's word for my soul

Date:

I'm thankful for...

Letting go of this anxious thought

Prayer focus & requests

Gratitude
Hopes
Dreams
Quotes
Verses
Poems
Lyrics
Thoughts
Messages

ReflectionS

Week#________

Today's word for my soul

Date:

I'm thankful for...

Letting go of this anxious thought

Prayer focus & requests

Today's word for my soul

Date:

I'm thankful for...

Letting go of this anxious thought

Prayer focus & requests

Today's word for my soul

Date:

I'm thankful for...

Letting go of this anxious thought

Prayer focus & requests

Today's word for my soul

Date:

I'm thankful for...

Letting go of this anxious thought

Prayer focus & requests

Today's word for my soul

Date:

I'm thankful for...

Letting go of this anxious thought

Prayer focus & requests

Today's word for my soul

Date:

I'm thankful for...

Letting go of this anxious thought

Prayer focus & requests

Gratitude
Hopes
Dreams
Quotes
Verses
Poems
Lyrics
Thoughts
Messages

ReflectionS

Week#_______

Today's word for my soul

Date:

I'm thankful for...

Letting go of this anxious thought

Prayer focus & requests

Today's word for my soul

Date:

I'm thankful for...

Letting go of this anxious thought

Prayer focus & requests

Today's word for my soul

Date:

I'm thankful for...

Letting go of this anxious thought

Prayer focus & requests

Today's word for my soul

Date:

I'm thankful for...

Letting go of this anxious thought

Prayer focus & requests

Today's word for my soul

Date:

I'm thankful for...

Letting go of this anxious thought

Prayer focus & requests

Today's word for my soul

Date:

I'm thankful for...

Letting go of this anxious thought

Prayer focus & requests

Gratitude
Hopes
Dreams
Quotes
Verses
Poems
Lyrics
Thoughts
Messages

ReflectionS

Week#_______

Rest,
Relax,
& Color

God has a bridge
called
Fear Not
That crosses over
my sea of anxieties

Quiet Time for the Bride-to-be

Delight yourself in
The Lord
and He shall give you
the desires of your heart.
Psalm 37:4

Quiet Time for the Bride-to-be

and it shall be given unto you...

and you shall find....

and the door shall be opened for you

Matthew 7:7

Quiet Time for the Bride-to-be

The
fervent
prayers
of
the
righteous
avails
much.
James 5:6

Quiet Time for the Bride-to-be

Be Thou
my vision
O Lord
of my life

Quiet Time for the Bride-to-be

Rejoice in the Lord
always
again I say
Rejoice
Philippians 4:4

Quiet Time for the Bride-to-be

I've been
BLESSED
to be a
Blessing

Quiet Time for the Bride-to-be

A cord of three strands
is not easily broken.

Ecclesiastes 4:12

Quiet Time for the Bride-to-be

Casting all
your care
upon
the Lord
because
He cares
for you.
1 Peter 5:7

Quiet Time for the Bride-to-be

BRIDE

to Be

God has made all things
beautiful in its time.

Ecclesiastes 3:11

Quiet Time for the Bride-to-be

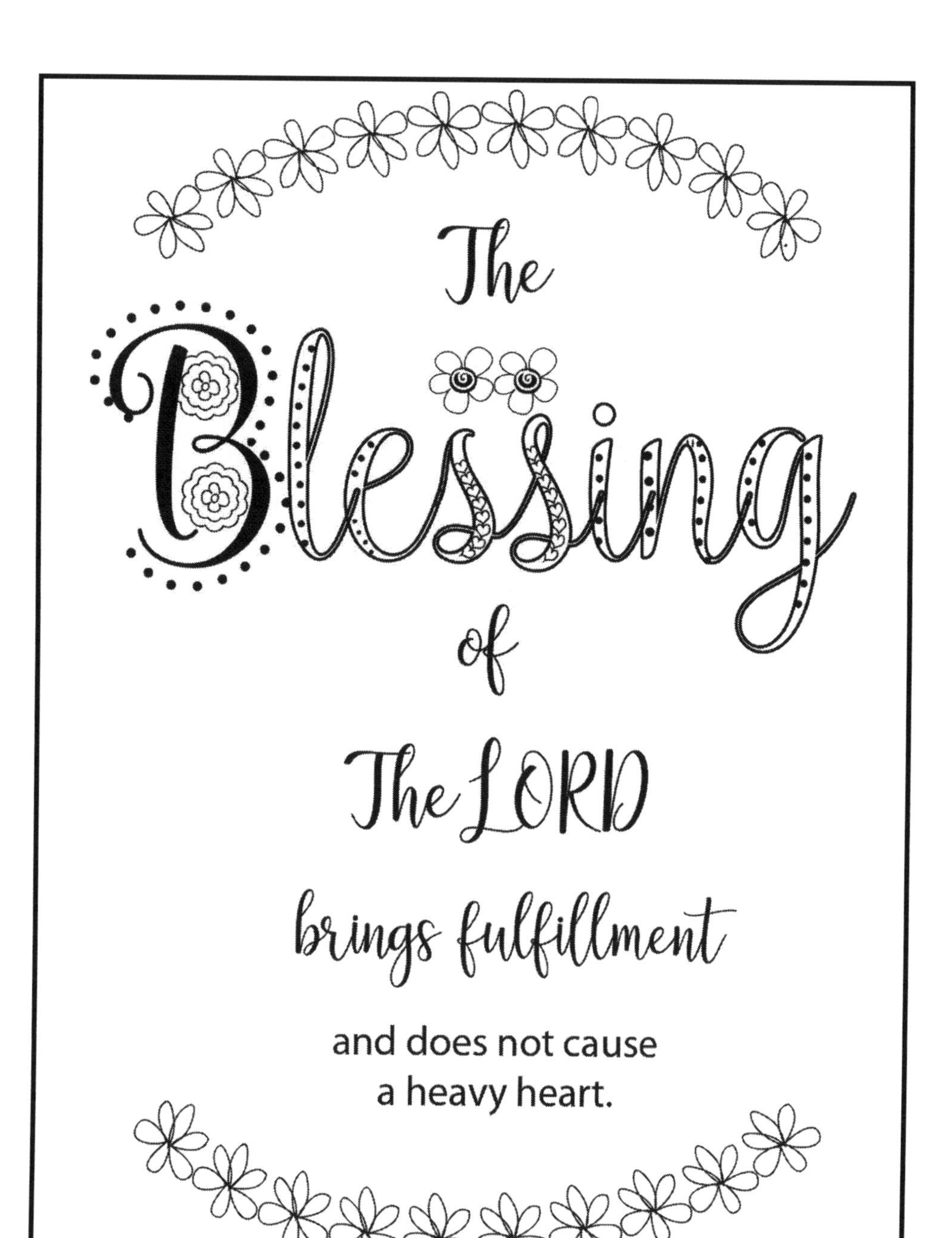

Proverbs 10:22

Quiet Time for the Bride-to-be

Satisfy us early
with
Your faithful love,
that we may
rejoice and be glad
all our days.
Psalm 90:14

Quiet Time for the Bride-to-be

I am my beloved's
and my
beloved is mine...

Song of Solomon 6:3

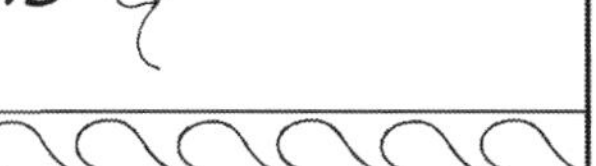

The Lord our God is with
us...He will take delight in
us...and rejoice over us with
singing.

Zephaniah 3:17

Quiet Time for the Bride-to-be

Be kind to each other,
tenderhearted, forgiving
one another, just as God,
for the sake of Christ,
has forgiven you.

Ephesians 4:32

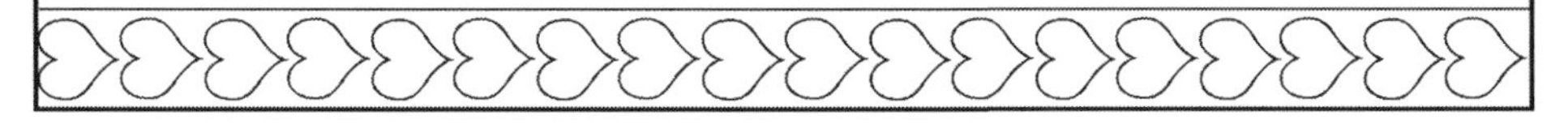

LIVE LOVE LAUGH

God's in control

Quiet Time for the Bride-to-be

"Inspired quotes"

Quiet Time for the Bride-to-be

“Inspired quotes”

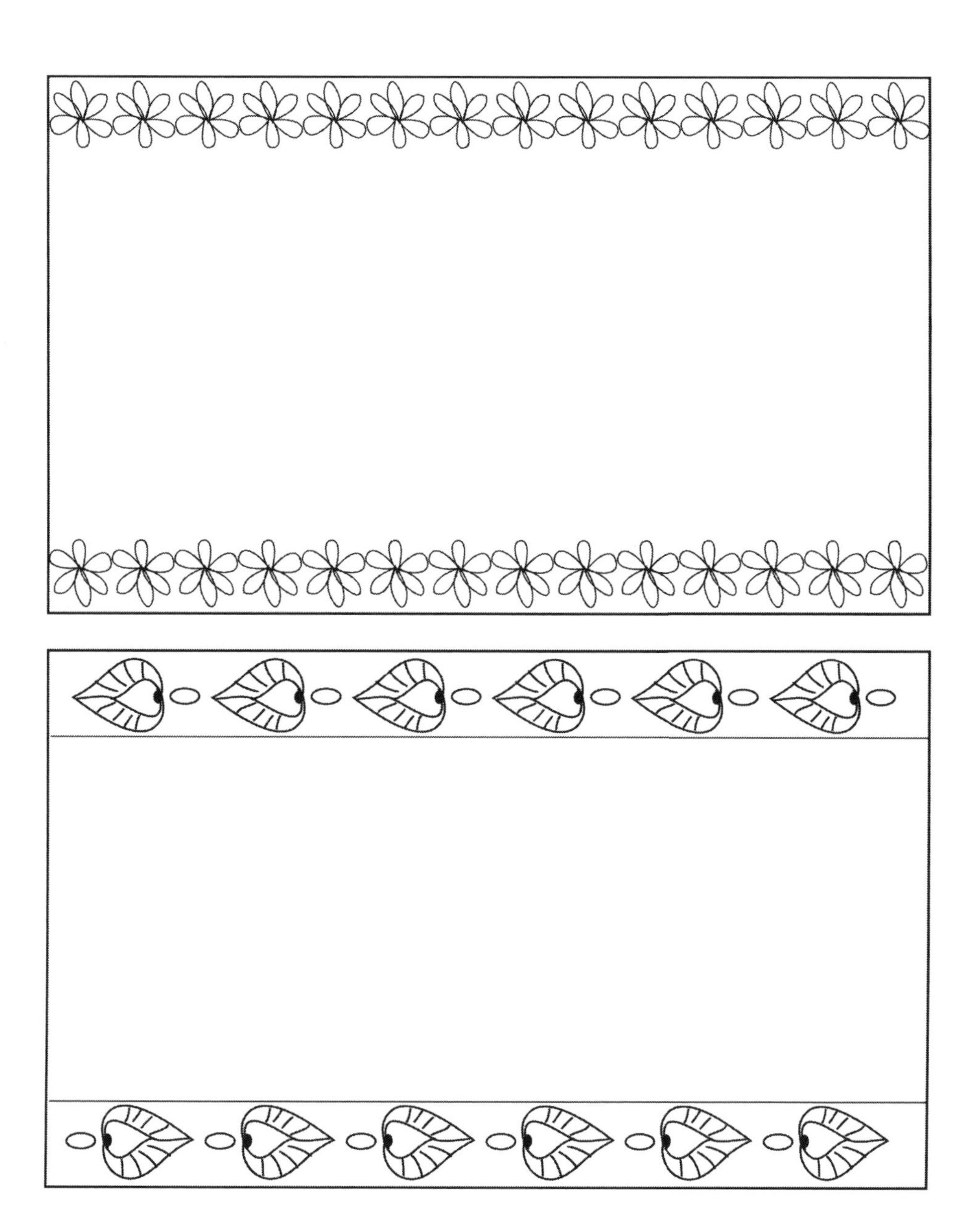